Regal
RUSSIAN BLUES

GRACEFUL! SHINY! LOVING!

SHY! INTELLIGENT! SENSITIVE!

ABDO
Publishing Company

Katherine Hengel

Consulting Editor, Diane Craig, M.A./Reading Specialist

visit us at www.abdopublishing.com

Published by ABDO Publishing Company, a division of ABDO, P.O. Box 398166, Minneapolis, Minnesota 55439. Copyright © 2012 by Abdo Consulting Group, Inc. International copyrights reserved in all countries. No part of this book may be reproduced in any form without written permission from the publisher. Super SandCastle™ is a trademark and logo of ABDO Publishing Company.

Printed in the United States of America, North Mankato, Minnesota
062011
092011

 PRINTED ON RECYCLED PAPER

Editor: Liz Salzmann
Content Developer: Nancy Tuminelly
Cover and Interior Design and Production:
   Anders Hanson, Mighty Media
Illustrations: Bob Doucet
Photo Credits: Shutterstock

Library of Congress Cataloging-in-Publication Data
Hengel, Katherine.
 Regal Russian blues / authored by Katherine Hengel ; illustrated by Bob Doucet.
   p. cm. -- (Cat craze set 2)
 ISBN 978-1-61714-832-3
 1. Russian Blue cat--Juvenile literature. I. Doucet, Bob, ill. II. Title.
 SF449.R86.H46 2012
 636.8'2--dc22
                          2010053269

CONTENTS

The Russian Blue	3
Facial Features	4
Body Basics	5
Coat & Color	6
Health & Care	8
Attitude & Behavior	10
Litters & Kittens	12
Buying a Russian Blue	14
Living with a Russian Blue	18
Komrade Kitty	20
Find the Russian Blue	22
The Russian Blue Quiz	23
Glossary	24

The
RUSSIAN BLUE

Russian blues are smart and **sensitive**. Their **unique** coats are famous! Their fur is a combination of blue, gray, and silver. In the cat world, this is called a blue coat. That's how the Russian blue got part of its name!

FACIAL FEATURES

Head

A Russian blue's head is medium sized. It's shaped like a wedge.

Muzzle

The Russian blue has a smooth **muzzle**. Its chin sticks out even with its nose.

Eyes

Their eyes are **emerald** green and set far apart.

Ears

Russian blues have large, triangular ears. The ears are far apart on the top of the head.

BODY BASICS

Size

Adult Russian blues weigh 8 to 12 pounds (4 to 6 kg).

Build

Russian blues have long, thin bodies. They have fine bones and strong **muscles**.

Tail

Russian blues have long tails. The ends of their tails are pointed.

Legs and Feet

Their legs are long and thick. Their paws are small and round.

COAT & COLOR

Russian Blue Fur

The Russian blue is famous for its coat. The fur is short and dense. It is a double coat. The undercoat is all one color. As you may have guessed, it's blue!

The Russian blue's guard hairs are the same length as the undercoat. They are blue with silver tips. The silver tips make the Russian blue's coat shine!

BLUE FUR

HEALTH & CARE

Life Span

Russian blues can live for more than 15 years!

Health Concerns

Russian blues are very healthy cats. They like to eat! It's important to make sure they don't eat too much.

VET'S CHECKLIST

- Have your Russian blue spayed or neutered. This will prevent unwanted kittens.

- Visit a vet for regular checkups.

- Ask your vet which types of food and litter are right for your Russian blue.

- Clean your Russian blue's teeth and ears once a week.

- Ask your vet about shots that may benefit your cat.

ATTITUDE & BEHAVIOR

Personality

Russian blues are intelligent and **sensitive**. They are **loyal** to their families. They often have a favorite family member! But Russian blues are shy around strangers. They like to be petted, but they don't need a lot of attention. They are quiet cats that can entertain themselves!

Activity Level

Russian blues are active. They like to climb and race around the house! They can even open doors and play fetch. They love learning new games.

All About Me

Hi! My name is Helga. I'm a Russian blue. I just wanted to let you know a few things about me. I made some lists below of things I like and dislike. Check them out!

Things I Like

- Playing with toys
- Being petted
- Playing fetch
- Climbing things
- Being with my owner
- Entertaining myself around the house

Things I Dislike

- Being around strangers
- Spending a lot of time alone
- Not having anything to play with

LITTERS & KITTENS

Litter Size

A female Russian blue usually gives birth to three to five kittens.

Diet

Newborn kittens drink their mother's milk. They can begin to eat kitten food when they are about six weeks old. Kitten food is different from cat food. It has the extra **protein**, fat, **vitamins**, and **minerals** that kittens need to grow.

Growth

Russian blues are born with blue eyes. As they grow up, their eyes turn green. Russian blue kittens should stay with their mothers until they are two to three months old. A Russian blue will be almost full grown when it is six months old. But it will continue to grow slowly until it is one year old.

BUYING A RUSSIAN BLUE

Choosing a Breeder

It's best to buy a kitten from a **breeder**, not a pet store. When you visit a cat breeder, ask to see the mother and father of the kittens. Make sure the parents are healthy, friendly, and well behaved.

Picking a Kitten

Choose a kitten that isn't too active or too shy. If you sit down, some of the kittens may come over to you. One of them might be the right one for you!

Is It the Right Cat for You?

Buying a cat is a big decision. You'll want to make sure your new pet suits your lifestyle.

Get out a piece of paper. Draw a line down the middle.

Read the statements listed here. Each time you agree with a statement from the left column, make a mark on the left side of your paper. When you agree with a statement from the right column, make a mark on the right side of your paper.

Quiet cats are great! ☐ ☐ I like cats that meow a lot.

It's okay if my cat climbs on things. ☐ ☐ I don't want my cat to climb all over things.

I want to be my cat's favorite person! ☐ ☐ I want a friendly cat that likes everyone.

I want an independent cat. ☐ ☐ Social cats that need a lot of attention are the best.

Short, shiny coats are awesome! ☐ ☐ Longhair cats are the best.

If you made more marks on the left side than on the right side, a Russian blue may be the right cat for you! If you made more marks on the right side of your paper, you might want to consider another breed.

Some Things You'll Need

Cats go to the bathroom in a **litter box**. It should be kept in a quiet place. Most cats learn to use their litter box all by themselves. You just have to show them where it is! The dirty **litter** should be scooped out every day. The litter should be changed completely every week.

Your cat's **food and water dishes** should be wide and shallow. This helps your cat keep its whiskers clean. The dishes should be in a different area than the litter box. Cats do not like to eat and go to the bathroom in the same area.

Cats love to scratch! **Scratching posts** help keep cats from scratching the furniture. The scratching post should be taller than your cat. It should have a wide, heavy base so it won't tip over.

Cats are natural predators. Without small animals to hunt, cats may become bored and unhappy. **Cat toys** can satisfy your cat's need to chase and capture. They will help keep your cat entertained and happy.

Cats should not play with balls of yarn or string. If they accidentally eat the yarn, they could get sick.

Cat claws should be trimmed regularly with special cat claw **clippers**. Regular nail clippers will also work. Some people choose to have their cat's claws removed by a vet. But most vets and animal rights groups think declawing is cruel.

You should brush your cat regularly with a **cat hair brush**. This will help keep its coat healthy and clean.

A **cat bed** will give your cat a safe, comfortable place to sleep.

LIVING WITH A RUSSIAN BLUE

Being a Good Companion

Russian blues are independent, but they like being with their owners. Spend time with your Russian blue. You'll build a great friendship! A Russian blue's fur doesn't need a lot of brushing. But many of them enjoy being brushed by their favorite person.

Inside or Outside?

It's a good idea to keep your Russian blue inside. Most vets and **breeders** agree that it is best for cats to be kept inside. That way the cats are safe from predators and cars.

18

Feeding Your Russian Blue

Russian blues may be fed regular cat food. Your vet can help you choose the best food for your cat.

Cleaning the Litter Box

Like all cats, Russian blues like to be clean. They don't like smelly or dirty litter boxes. If the litter box is dirty, they may go to the bathroom somewhere else. Ask your vet for advice if your cat isn't using its box.

☠ DANGER:
POISONOUS FOODS

Some people like to feed their cats table scraps. Here are some human foods that can make cats sick.

TOMATOES

POTATOES

ONIONS

GARLIC

CHOCOLATE

GRAPES

KOMRADE KITTY

Russian blues are from northern Russia near the Arctic Circle. Their thick coats helped them survive in the cold. Some say they were once hunted for their fur. Maybe that's why Russian blues are still **wary** of strangers!

20

In the late 1800s, Russian blues were brought onto trade ships. The ships sailed to England from Arkhangelsk, Russia. Arkhangelsk was a major port. This is why Russian blues are often called Archangel blues.

FIND THE RUSSIAN BLUE

A

B

C

D

THE RUSSIAN BLUE QUIZ

1. Russian blues are smart and **sensitive**. **True or false?**

2. Russian blues have **emerald** green eyes. **True or false?**

3. Russian blues have long and thin fur. **True or false?**

4. Russian blues are not very healthy cats. **True or false?**

5. Russian blues often have a favorite family member! **True or false?**

6. Russian blues are also called Archangel blues. **True or false?**

Answers: 1) true 2) true 3) false 4) false 5) true 6) true

GLOSSARY

breed – a group of animals or plants with common ancestors. A *breeder* is someone whose job is to breed certain plants or animals.

dense – thick or crowded together.

emerald – a bright green color.

loyal – faithful or devoted to someone or something.

mineral – a natural element that plants, animals, and people need to be healthy.

muscle – the tissue connected to the bones that allows body parts to move.

muzzle – the nose and jaws of an animal.

protein – a substance found in all plant and animal cells.

sensitive – easily affected by something seen, heard, or felt.

unique – unusual or special.

vitamin – a substance needed for good health, found naturally in plants and meats.

wary – careful, cautious, and watchful.